What Others Are Saying about This Book...

"One of the many wonderful features of this book is that it helps teens feel as though they are not alone in facing the tumultuous time of adolescence. Jennifer has certainly built a case for the glow that only knowing and understanding yourself can illuminate and has given teens the tools to 'buff up' the inside, as well as the outside. Warm, witty, and welcome advice from a writer who knows how to get the message across to teenagers in language they can understand and appreciate. Teens will love this book!" —**Suzee Vlk, J.D.author,** *SAT for Dummies*

"A must for every teenager!"—**Cathy Schmachtenberger, Books Are Fun**

"After reading this book, I'm no longer comparing myself to others. I'm feeling more comfortable in my own skin." —**Suzanne Reeves, 16**

"This book showed me that I didn't have to feel bad about myself when someone drops me as their friend. I've learned that when you believe in yourself, you feel strong. I love that idea. Trusting myself and believing in me makes me a beautiful person to be around!"—**Mya Adams, 14**

"As Jennifer says, 'You can't always change the things that make you look stressed, but you can change the way you react to them.' I like that idea, a lot!" —**Priscilla Dillon, 18**

"This book is very reassuring to a teen's sense of self." —**Tanya Jamal, 16**

"Traversing adolescence can be tricky, especially as it pertains to having confidence in one's appearance. This wonderful guide written for young people shows them how to attain a positive sense of self and to care for themselves. Very informative, practical and easy to digest."
—**Miriam Lodell, Michigan high-school educator**

CONFIDENCE & SELF-ESTEEM
FOR TEENS

Jennifer Leigh Youngs
co-author of the *Taste Berries for Teens* series and the *Taste Berries for Teens Journal*

Foreword by Bettie B. Youngs, Ph.D., Ed.D.
co-author of the *Taste Berries for Teens* series

burres books

Copyright © 2014 Jennifer Leigh Youngs and Bettie B. Youngs

All rights reserved. No part of this publication may be reproduced, stored in a retrieval system or transmitted in any form or by any means, electronic, mechanical, photocopying, recording or otherwise, without the written permission of the publisher.

Burres Books is an imprint of Bettie Youngs Book Publishers Co., Inc.

If you are unable to order this book from your local bookseller, or online from *Amazon* or *Barnes & Noble,* or from Wholesaler *Baker & Taylor,* or from *Espresso,* or *Read How You Want,* you may order directly from the publisher: Sales@BettieYoungs.com.

ISBN trade paper: 978-1-940784-35-9
ISBN ebook: 978-1-940784-34-2

Library of Congress Catalogue Control Number: 2014947377

1. Adolescence. 2. Self-Esteem—Juvenile literature. 3. Beauty, Personal, Juvenile literature. 4. Body image in adolescence—Juvenile literature. 5. Self-Confidence. 6. Goal Setting. 7. Imagination. 8. Dreaming. 9. Careers. 10. Bettie Youngs Books. 11. Burres Books. 12. Confidence.

Also by Jennifer Leigh Youngs:

✺ Taste Berries for Teens: Inspirational Short Stories and Encouragement on Life, Love, Friendship and Tough Issues

✺ Taste Berries for Teens Journal: My Thoughts on Life, Love and Making a Difference

✺ More Taste Berries for Teens: A Second Collection of Inspirational Stories and Encouragement on Life, Love, Friendship and Tough Issues

✺ Taste Berries for Teens #3: Inspirational Stories and Encouragement on Life, Love, Friends and the Face in the Mirror

✺ Taste Berries for Teens #4: Short Stories and Encouragement on Being Cool, Caring and Courageous

✺ A Taste Berry Teen's Guide to Setting & Achieving Goals

✺ A Taste Berry Teen's Guide to Managing the Stress and Pressures of Life

✺ 12 Months of Faith: A Devotional Journal for Teens

✺ 365 Days of Taste-Berry Inspiration for Teens

✺ A Teen's Guide to Christian Living

✺ A Teen's Guide to Living Drug-Free

✺ Moments and Milestones Pregnancy Journal

✺ 7 Ways a Baby Will Change Your Life

CONTENTS

Foreword by Bettie B. Youngs i
About This Book v

1. If Only I Had Known in High School
What I Know Now! 1
The Priceless Qualities That Make a Girl Sizzle with Appeal | Fice Secrets of Inner Beauty | Are You the Ultimate "Drama-Mama"? | How to Have Grace Under Pressure | Why and How Beauty Begins on the Inside

2. The Radiance of Inner Beauty 9
Why Nature Is Good for Your Heart and Soul | The Most Perfect Expression of Beauty: Feeling at Peace Within Ourselves | Soul Food—Feeding the Source of Inner Strength and Guidance | Creative Ways to Eavesdrop on the Universe | How to Be Genuinely Happy and Content

3. The Picture of Self-Esteem 15
The "Me" of Me: The Importance of Your Self-Esteem | How Your Self-Esteem Creates a Picture of Your Beauty | What You Can Do to Improve Your Self-Esteem | "Just Me, Love Dan" | Self-Esteem: Building Beauty from the Inside Out | The Benefits of a Healthy Self-Esteem | How to Change Your Self-Esteem

4. From "Me" to "You" 25

It Takes Two to Tango: How Harmony with Others Creates Inner Beauty | The Bunny-Love Experiment: Getting—and Giving—All the TLC You Need | Why Helping Others Feel Good About Themselves Will Make You Feel Better About Yourself | How to Have Great Relationships with Friends, Family and Others

5. The Beauty of Purpose and Passion 33
How to Be Smart, Sassy, Classy and in Charge of Yourself | Meet Patricia Hill Burnett—Proof that Talent, Skill and Important Work Give Meaning to Your Life | A Goal Is Like a Road Map—How to Set and Achieve Your Own

Other Books for Young Adults 39

FOREWORD

Dear Teen Reader,

Being a teenager is an exciting—and confusing—time. You feel on top of the world one day, and down in the dumps the next. You feel self-confident one day, only be greeted by self-doubt the next. You look in the mirror and feel quite sure that you are positively looking like hot stuff and then, before you know it, your great-hair day, your radiant complexion and your good mood take a drastic U-turn. Who needs it?

Adolescence is like that. But no one needs to tell you about the pros and cons of being a teen. So instead, let me tell you a little about the author of this book. Her name is Jennifer Leigh Youngs and she is my daughter. When she was born, she looked and behaved like most babies: she was cute, had very wrinkled skin, scowled a lot, and her screaming for food terrified the family dog. I love her beyond words and have always wanted the best for her, but even so, she had to deal with life like everyone else: day-by-day.

She was a cute little girl, but by fourth grade was feeling "oblong and ugly." Having looked like Cinderella throughout much of her childhood, she wondered out loud how nature could have dealt her such a cruel blow. Now she was gangly and uncoordinated, her facial features were elongating and filling out—and not all at the same time. She was really upset about it. She complained and complained, and no reassurance on my part could appease her.

One day Jennifer and I were going through a box of old pictures and came across all my childhood pictures that my mother had kept for me. Jennifer was very interested in these old photos—one more so than the others. The particular photo that caught her attention was one of me with an extraordinarily goofy grin on my face, oversized front teeth and the two on either side of them missing. As she described it, I looked like the "Ultimate Geek." She flipped the photo over and there, in my mother's beautiful handwriting, was, "Bettie in fourth grade." My daughter rolled on the floor with laughter!

With a better understanding that a picture is worth a thousand words, I gathered up my childhood photos, arranged them in a year-by-year chronology, then had them put into one large frame. I hung this array of photos in the hallway outside her room. My daughter visited these photos quite often over the years, most especially when she was in her teens. I have no doubt that they helped her accept that with each year comes a new and different "look"—and perhaps helped her gain a little tolerance for all the changes she was going through, both physically and emotionally. At least I'd like to think so.

One day when she was in the tenth grade, my daughter asked, "Mom, when you were a sophomore, did anyone ask you to the junior-senior prom?" I thought she was warming up to ask me if she could accept a date to go to the junior-senior prom. But, when I replied, "No, no such luck," she remarked, "It probably had something to do with how 'nerdy' you looked in that phase!" Then, upon reviewing an assortment of other photos of me during my high school years, Jennifer remarked, "Mom, you sure did change a lot from year to year. How is it possible to be so cool one year and nerdy the next?"

Adolescence is like that. So many changes, inside and out. Different looks, different feelings.

What Jennifer learned and wants you to understand is that much of what you see and how you feel during the teen years belongs to a "stage of development," albeit an intense one. But keep in mind that all of us, at every age in our lives, are in a constant process of changing. Most of us may like our appearance a great deal one year, and the next only so-so. Or, we may be quite happy with the results of one stage, and wish we could skip other changes altogether!

Maybe right now you are going through a great phase—one in which you are healthy and happy and feeling good about yourself. Maybe your body feels energized rather than lazy from all the growing and hormonal changes going on. If so, great! But if you aren't feeling quite like

Cinderella at the ball, remember that it's just that, a phase. Just ask your parents; they know from experience. I'll bet they have some photos of themselves much like those Jennifer discovered of me—photos that showed them in various stages of looking hot, and in Jennifer's words for me in tenth grade, "nerdy." We all change, especially in the teen years. As Jason, one of Jennifer's friends, said to me, "I look totally different than I did just three months ago because then I had a decent complexion, and now it's oily and zit-ridden. Then I had a great physique; now my body parts look like they don't belong with the other parts. Now, from one day to the next, my emotions are all over the place. Everything is changing! I'm looking forward to the time when the real me will stay around long enough for me to get used to!"

For Jason, it may be awhile. He just turned fifteen! But even though adolescence is a time of many changes—and some of them, like extra-oily skin you'd like to do without—there are some things you can do to feel good and look great while your body is moving from this stage to the next. This practical health, fitness and beauty guide can help you look and feel attractive, inside and out, as you go through the tumultuous time of adolescence and help you answer questions that practically every teenager asks: What's with my ever-changing emotions and feelings? How can I understand them, much less cope? How can I look great all the time—even when I'm feeling so not "with it"? How can I feel self-confident and sure of myself when I'm not as attractive as others? How can I fit in, be one of the "cool" kids? What is the best way to care for my skin and hair, especially now that it's extra oily? How can I look great? What are the secrets of "cool"? What can I do to make the most of my looks, my body, my appearance?

These and a million other questions are asked by teens the world over. It's only natural to want to look and feel your best. There are practical benefits as well. Liking the way you look and feel can be a real edge in helping you be yourself around others. The more authentic you are—the more you stay true to the person you are—the less likely you will compromise yourself or your values to gain approval and acceptance from others. Having taught both junior and senior high school—not to mention having a house full of teenagers when my daughter was an adolescent—I have a better appreciation for the ups and downs teens go through in this incredible time of growth, and especially for how tough it can be to go through this stage with other teens! As teens compare themselves to their peers, they often judge each other harshly and can be cruel in their remarks to each other. The more you like and accept yourself, the more confident you will be in keeping these comments in perspective; this can take the sting out of having your feelings hurt.

My daughter has blossomed out of her gangly phase and has become a lovely young woman. Like many of her classmates, she breezed through some phases, and grumbled and mumbled her way through others. Jennifer, now twenty-five, is a soulful person—one who sees people and life through the eyes of her heart. She has an eye for beauty, a nose for common sense and an extraordinarily large funny bone. She is a young woman who is comfortable in her own skin, and would love for you to be, too. Her advice in this book is simple: Value your health and do not sacrifice it. Believe in yourself and make friends with the face in the mirror. Have the courage to be an individual; be aware of others around you; be friendly and courteous, but don't forget that you are you. Appreciate yourself; learn to enjoy the feeling of being healthy, fit and attractive on your terms. Be as healthy, fit and beautiful as you can be—but never lose sight of the fact that you get to decide what that means for you. Offer up your brand of beauty; you are who the world is waiting to see and learn all about.

If you will take this advice, you will reach the same happy conclusion as Jennifer: With each year there is a growing sense of self-confidence in your own style and in your own individual beauty. While we live in a world filled with others, we are each one-of-a-kind. Love that person, and we will, too. **—Bettie B. Youngs, Ph.D., Ed.D.**

ABOUT THIS BOOK

Confidence & Self-Esteem for Teens is about the ways that beauty manifests from within. Have you ever run across someone who looked pretty, but undid her beauty by the way she acted or treated others? Compare that to someone who is thoughtful and has a kind heart, confident and comfortable with herself and as a result, has a lovely presence about her. What is the difference between lovely and beautiful? The difference is inner harmony—and it's a huge part of true beauty.

This book shows you how to let your inner beauty shine through—things like the secrets of serenity, steps for staying cool under pressure, building your self-esteem, drawing security from loving others, setting goals and feeling purposeful—and more.

1
If Only I Had Known in High School What I Know Now!

Life is a challenge—Meet it!
Life is a song—Sing it!
Life is a dream—Realize it!
Life is a game—Play it!
Life is love—Enjoy it!
—Sri Sathya Sai Baba

Beauty Begins on the Inside

One of the things I liked best—and least—about being a teenager was the excitement of things being so "do or die!" For me, every little thing—every single word, action and even the thoughts of my family and friends (of course I always just knew what they were thinking)—was crucial, urgent and dire. For example, when I was in high school, if I wanted to go out with a certain guy, I hoped, planned and prayed that he would ask me out. I worried one minute that he wouldn't ask and worried the next minute what I would do or say if and when he did. Then, when the guy did ask me out, I fretted that I somehow wouldn't measure up to his previous girlfriend—who I always pictured as drop-dead gorgeous, popular with everyone with whom she came into contact, brilliant and talented, and with a great body that was buffed to the max. Never mind that I didn't know her, nor had I ever even seen her.

Never mind that I was a good athlete, was often on the honor roll and had many good friends. Somehow, I never really figured out that I could compete on my own merits. I worried about everything. Everything was such a big deal.

The Ultimate "Drama-Mama"

As agonizing as all this was, I didn't let it interfere with my being even more of a "drama-mama." On the day of the big date, I would be simply devastated if my hair wasn't exactly perfect, if my complexion wasn't as clear as I hoped it would be; or if I didn't feel that I looked exactly as spectacular as I wanted. Then, even though my date and I had a nice time on that first date, I next worried about whether or not my heartthrob would ask me out again. When he did, I wondered if—and when—we would have date three, four, and five. You get the idea.

When the boyfriend became "my guy," getting-a-guy anxiety gave way to keeping-my-guy anxiety. Now the task in my head was to make sure everyone knew Romeo and I were a "solid" couple, that our soulmate-love-made-in-heaven was forever, so they better "stay off my turf."

Of course, the guy was probably going through a similar charade as well, one complete with its own doubts and insecurities. But I didn't let that limit me from having fears of my own. The more the merrier!

So whether it was guys, grades, good friends or the way I looked and dressed, I put myself through the paces. Everything was "do or die."

Brad Wilson: "To Die For"

I'm older now, but even so, I still have my share of anxiety-ridden situations, only now things no longer seem so "do or die!" Experience has taught me to take things in stride and to trust myself more. And this trust makes all the difference in the world. For example, six months ago I met a great-looking guy (Brad Wilson) who asked me out for the following Saturday night. We agreed he'd pick me up at seven o'clock.

I was really looking forward to going out with Brad. On each of the several occasions I'd talked with him prior to his asking me out, I found him to be stylish, smart and savvy, funny, and as we would say in high school, "cool" and "to die for." So when the Saturday arrived, I bounded out of bed and headed for work in a better mood than usual (I work every other Saturday from 10:00 to 5:00). I was really looking forward to the evening. The day flew by!

Because I was off work at five o'clock, I knew I'd have ample time to run the two errands I needed to get done: picking up my hot new blazer and skirt from the cleaners so I could wear them on my date with Brad, and stopping at the city library to pick up a research book for an important college term paper due the following Monday. My brain had a time schedule all worked out: off at 5:00, to the cleaners by 5:15, at the library at 5:30, home by 6:00. Once at home, I'd do a quick twenty-minute pick-me-up workout with my favorite workout video to reenergize, then put on my favorite CD, take a relaxing bubble bath and have thirty minutes to dress for my big date!

Regardless of my being organized, things didn't go as planned! It fact, it took only ten minutes for things to begin to unravel! The employee who takes over when I leave at 5:00 called in sick. I found this out when the store manager phoned me and asked if I would please stay until he came in to cover for the sick employee. Of course, I said I would.

The manager said he would be at the store in twenty minutes—only he didn't arrive until 5:50!

Getting off work at 5:50 instead of 5:00 really cut into the time I'd planned for the leisurely and relaxed evening before my date arrived. Nevertheless, I left work the instant my manager arrived and headed straight for the cleaners, only to discover that the cleaners had already closed for the day. Although this was upsetting, I headed immediately to the library. I couldn't skip this errand because the city library is closed on Sundays, so I had no option but to go check out the book I needed for the paper I'd planned to do the next day. At least I thought I'd be checking out the book. When I got to the library, I found that the book hadn't been returned!

In short, not only were things not going as planned, but I was running very late. So late that I arrived home only minutes before my "to die for" date arrived!

Grace Under Pressure

If something similar had happened to me as a teenager, I would have been beside myself, working myself into a frenzy. Then I would have been in a bad mood, and who knows what kind of an evening I would have created. But now I'm learning to relax a bit, to take things in stride, and to work with each situation—especially those that require grace under pressure. So when Brad knocked at the door, I opened it and said politely, "It's wonderful to see you. I'm running about twenty minutes late. Come in and make yourself comfortable. If we need to reschedule dinner reservations, the phone is in the kitchen. I'll tell you all about it over dinner!"

Then, twenty minutes later, Brad and I left my apartment and went to dinner. My hair was not having the best of days, and I was not wearing the hot new blazer and skirt that I had hoped to wear. Even so, I made the best of it and selected my next-favorite outfit. As upsetting as it was that the research book I had planned on using for my term paper had not been returned to the library like it was supposed to have been, I decided I'd have to figure out a contingency plan the next day. I didn't have the benefit of reenergizing after a long day at work, or the benefit of relaxation time so as to switch gears from the "mental briefcase" of work-related problems. And the much-desired bubble bath where I had intended to dreamily anticipate the evening with Brad . . . well, that went down the drain (!) as well.

From "Ghoul" to "Cool"

I've learned that when things don't go as planned, when they aren't exactly the way you'd like them to be, you have to make the best of what you have. When you're stressed out or worrying about every little thing, it takes away from your "cool"—from looking and acting "together." With my new date, I simply had to get comfortable with the fact that I'd had a particularly hectic day and make the decision that I wasn't going to drag it along with me to dinner with Brad.

If only I had known in high school what I know now, I could have saved myself a lot of undue stress and looked a lot more cool to boot.

The secret of getting from A to B—from drama-mama to cool—is this: You can't always control the outer world, but you can control how you respond—how you act—in relation to what's going on around you. Unlike those things that you have little say or control over, such as the natural color of your eyes or an occasional bad hair day, the qualities that radiate your cool are under your control. Those qualities include a positive attitude and a decision to remain calm and focus on the solutions, rather than the problems at hand. Just as you put on an outfit that looks hot on you, or wear your hair in a style that compliments your face, or wear fingernail polish, lipstick or mascara to add color and pizzazz, you can greatly enhance the color of your cool. It's a choice you make to draw control from within. This choice becomes visible in a poised beauty that shines through you.

A Secret of Inner Beauty: "Act" Beautiful

You carry your beauty with you every minute of every day, every place you go. I'll never forget the evening when a small group of us were returning from touring several of the old Southern plantations in Charleston, South Carolina, where we were attending Renaissance Weekend. A four-day event, Renaissance days began bright and early at seven o'clock. After the plantation tours, we went to dinner. After a ten-hour conference, then touring and dinner, I don't mind telling you, I was dragging!

It was nearly 11:30 at night, and I was slouched in the small transport van in the seat beside eighty-year-old Patricia Hill Burnett. Exhausted and bleary-eyed, I gazed over at Patricia, sitting perfectly erect. Her chin up, she looked poised and lovely, every bit like a grand Southern belle. "Aren't you tired?" I inquired, puzzled by her apparently endless energy and the fact that she could still look so composed, refreshed and beautiful after the day we'd had. "I'm exhausted," I said, "and quite sure I look it. But you look so fresh and perky, as though you've napped. Have you?"

"Oh, no," she replied, admitting, "It's been quite a long day and I am most definitely tired."

"But you look so radiant, so beautiful," I remarked. "I've used up my allotment for the day. How do you do it?"

With her customary warmth and tenderness, Patricia reached for my hand, looked me in the eyes, and in her style of speaking while at the same time smiling, pointed to her head and said sweetly, "I keep a little reserve of beauty right up here." Laughing softly, she added, "You are only as beautiful as you feel on the inside. Beauty is from the inside out. And, just as they say about sunshine, you have to carry it with you! To be beautiful, you must act beautiful."

Patricia's radiance comes not only from being beautiful, but also from acting beautiful. It's one of the great secrets of beauty: Beauty comes from within.

It is primarily from this vantage point—beauty from the inside out—that we are beautiful.

Like Money in the Bank: The Glow of Inner Beauty

Inner beauty has a powerful glow, one that is clearly visible to those around you. Perhaps you know someone like my friend, Patricia, whose inner beauty shines so brightly you describe her as "a beautiful person." Unfortunately, some people are beautiful outside . . . and not so pretty inside. Perhaps you know someone who possesses great physical beauty but whose lack of inner vibrancy overshadows or even cancels out her outer beauty.

I'm reminded of a young man who wrote telling me he'd met a girl he thought was the "most beautiful girl he had ever seen." Finally he got up the courage to ask her out. When she accepted, he thought he was the luckiest guy in the world. The feeling was short-lived. As he began to get to know her, he saw a person who was very different from what he had imagined. He discovered the girl wasn't very kind and respectful of other people, qualities he associated with her not being happy within herself. After dating her for only five weeks, the young man decided not to ask the girl out anymore. "Seeing her beauty, I thought she must be beautiful," he wrote, "but as I got to see the real person, I could tell that her beauty was all on the outside, just an outward appearance. Even that wasn't lasting: When she didn't have her makeup on, she didn't think she was pretty and it showed in the way she treated others. I've learned that if a person doesn't feel pretty on the inside, then even though she is beautiful to look at, the advantage is shallow. When inner beauty is missing, your feelings of attraction for that person wear off. Being pretty on the outside can only get you so far."

So how do you acquire inner beauty? It's not elusive. As this unit will show you, acquiring inner beauty is largely about:

- Drawing inspiration from the sources that tie us to timeless truths.
- Developing a positive sense of self.
- Interacting with others in positive ways.
- Knowing what you want out of life and having purposeful goals.
- Managing your response to stress.
- Caring for yourself by keeping yourself healthy and fit.
- So how did things turn out with my "to die for" date? Great! At the end of a really nice evening, I said simply, "Thank you for being so patient with me this evening." My date was impressed with my "cool"—and so was I.

2

The Radiance of Inner Beauty

People are like stained glass windows. They sparkle and shine when the sun is out; but when the darkness sets in their true beauty is revealed only if there is a light inside. —Elisabeth Kübler-Ross

Nature—Good for Your Heart and Soul

I love to go bike riding with my friends because biking is good exercise and a great way to spend time with them. But another reason is that being outdoors, being in the midst of nature is good for my heart and soul. Nature can help us get in touch with the bigger world we live in.

Picture that you and several of your best friends have ridden your bikes to the top of a steep hill, where you stop to rest. You look into a vast blue horizon where clouds that look like tufts of cotton balls lounge like lazy alligators sunning on a river bank on a hot summer's day. You look down into an immense valley of lush green trees and hearty ground-shrubs sprinkled with patches of wildflowers, a picturesque landscape—a sharp contrast to the teeny-tiny flowers decorating the ground beneath your feet.

You are filled with an appreciation for the wonder and beauty of nature, one that leaves you with a feeling of awe and serenity.

As though she notices your appreciation—perhaps by your tranquil smile or from the lengthy breath of fresh mountain air you've drawn deep into your lungs—Mother Nature, having already flaunted her beauty, decides to please you even more. Intricately colored butterflies flutter to and fro and from flower to flower, each exquisite bloom generously offering up its sweet fragrance. Bees buzz by, busily sampling the sweet nectar and carrying it off to distant places. As though to compliment the phenomenal array of activity going on around you, a medley of tunes begins to play: You hear the clicking and chatter of busy-bodied chipmunks and bushy-tailed ground squirrels as they scurry about foraging for food. Birds cheerfully chirp, their medley of happiness as evident as that of the other multitude of inhabitants of this hill who, though unseen, make their presence known.

In this moment, all call out to each other. What a choir!

You can't help but feel the powerful stirrings going on inside of you. You marvel at all this intoxicating splendor, and ponder what it must be like to be a butterfly, willfully following a sweet scent, or a bird free to surf the warm winds. You feel a kinship with all the other little creatures making their way through the day, most especially that little rodent playing hide-and-seek with the shadow overhead in hopes he doesn't become a hungry hawk's timely, tasty lunch.

Inner Peace—The Most Perfect Expression of Beauty

These are precious moments. In such moments we can't help but grasp that we live in a universe buzzing and humming with life—a life force in which all beings are dependent upon each other.

These moments are insightful. In these moments wherein the gentle whistling of the wind speaks louder than the laughter of friends or the experience of our victories and defeats, intuitively we are reminded to "drink in" the knowledge that our heart, mind, body and soul are at this moment "one"—and perfect.

And these moments are sacred. Lost in time, we are reunited with truths larger and more profound than events in our everyday lives. We live in a world of creation, one where a universal energy permeates all living matter. What a shame if we don't grasp the importance of being in harmony with that which is all around us.

Though your friends call out to you, as much as you love being in their presence, human words intrude on the power of this feeling of completeness. You realize this feeling is the best! It can hardly be improved upon. Having more friends, getting a new outfit, even having more dollars in your wallet—all seem unnecessary in this moment. A new hairstyle, or the latest shade of lipstick or nail polish cannot brighten your outlook more than the glow you feel when all is well on the inside.

Feeling complete, being at peace within, is the most perfect expression of beauty.

The Fountain of True Inner Beauty

I believe with all my heart that the feeling of being at peace and complete is an outcome of our faith. Faith is the eternal spring from which true inner beauty flows. One of the most beautiful women I've ever seen is Heather Whitestone, Miss America 1995—a shining example of the power of this spring. Devout in her faith and certain that her calling is to witness to the purpose of it, her deep inner harmony shines outwardly in a joy that leaps from her face to your heart. It is the innocent beauty of her soul, created by the anchor of her faith, that you see even before you notice Heather's striking physical beauty. Perhaps you have seen her on television commercials or speaking to youth around the country. Once you've seen this exquisite woman, you will never, ever forget her. Her outer beauty is undeniably breathtaking. But it is her inner radiance that is so incredibly captivating to the point that she is simply unforgettable.

One on One—Alone or in a Crowd

Being together, talking, laughing and just sharing is a common experience that affirms we are a part of the greater whole of the human race. But just as we are a part of a vast human civilization, like a single star among the vast galaxy wherein each star has its own force to play out, we each journey through time alone, and we each experience it in our own way. We humans are each a single soul in search of meaning. We must feed our hearts. As much as we like and need our friends, no amount of exciting times with them can compensate or take the place of finding the meaning of our own existence. Even when with others, we experience our lives one-on-one. We will each encounter times in our lives when we are faced with challenges we must cope with all alone.

Acknowledging a one-on-one relationship with a force greater than ourselves is the foundation of faith. Faith can provide us with leadership and strength, drawing upon sources that inspire and uplift us, as they tie us to the timeless truths of all humanity, truths that in our souls we know to be so.

The Source of Inner Strength and Guidance

An unending source of joy and peace, this ever available faith is also a source of strength and guidance—an anchor that sustains us not only when all is going well, but especially when we feel alone or overwhelmed. It offers comfort when no one else can—as many teens in the Columbine massacre discovered when for more than three hours they holed up in Columbine's choir office. Facing a terrorist wasn't the first time seventeen-year-old Cassie Bernall drew upon her faith. Once a troubled teen who did drugs, her faith became her reason for turning from the despair of drugs and helped her realign her life toward a purpose. Countless others have found this to be true as well. At the heart of most Twelve Step recovery programs, such as Al-Anon, Alcoholics Anonymous and others like them, spiritual principles stand as a point of hope to acquire the strength and direction to achieve and maintain freedom from destructive behavior. Experts have found that it is only by surrendering to the unconditional love of a Higher Power that most people "recovering" from serious addictions are able to live freely.

Soul Food: Your Faith

Because faith is so central to our wholeness, and it is this wholeness that gives us this inner harmony, a harmony that radiates from the inside out, we need to care for this vital source of genuine beauty. Your spiritual self needs nourishment.

Whatever your faith, feed your heart and soul by studying the doctrines of your religion and applying their meaning to your everyday life. Don't worry that you will be considered a prude. Just the opposite is true. Modeling faith is uplifting and inspirational to others. The example of Cassie Bernall's witnessing of her faith on that tragic last day of her life in Littleton, Colorado, galvanized teens nationwide to think about faith and its role in their lives. Rallies within nearly thirty states are now underway for teens to ponder their own respective faith and ways to serve it. Countless Internet sites are now devoted to teen faith, and fresh, new songs are penned heralding the role of faith in our lives.

Eavesdrop on the Universe: Experience the Mysterious

We may not always understand the workings of faith, but that doesn't make it any less real or valuable. Albert Einstein said, "The most beautiful thing we can experience is the mysterious." Sometimes faith is found in just such mysterious experiences. Check it out for yourself:

- Eavesdrop on the way the universe silently breathes its wonders into life. Plant three different kinds of flowers. Water them. Observe them as they grow. Notice how different and intricate each bloom is. Enjoy their beauty. Notice how a dry seed willfully grows into a thing of delicate beauty. Appreciate the mystery of life.

- Eavesdrop on the way the universe pulses with love. Watch the eyes of someone light up when they speak about someone they love. Observe the obvious joy and love of parents of a newborn when they talk about their baby. Watch the searing emotions apparent in the eyes of parents as they describe the joys and victories—or the trials, tribulations and defeats—of their teenager. Notice how deeply protective the bonds of love are. Marvel at the depth and power of such passion.

- Eavesdrop on the still, quiet way the universe unites you to all life. Contemplate the tug you've felt inside your heart to offer a smile to a stranger, to speak softly to a pet, to help someone in trouble, or to be kind, or simply to do the right thing. Why this feeling and what is its source? Then think of how good it made you feel when you responded to that inner calling. Recall the sense of purpose, of value and connection this contact and response ultimately brought you. Reflect on the mysterious unity that exists in being part of a much greater whole.

Believe that your life has a purpose, and that you have something to contribute. You are valued, wanted and needed. Allow your faith to nourish you in all times, good as well as difficult. Feel the power of it in your life. It is a potent source of a most radiant and luminous beauty.

3

The Picture of Self-Esteem

Health comes from learning to live in vibrant harmony with ourselves, with the natural world, and with one another. —John Robbins

The "Me" of Me

Have you noticed how some people are very comfortable being themselves? LeAnna Simons, one of my really good friends, is that way. People are always remarking, "LeAnna has such a nice 'presence' about her, such a positive 'sense of self.'" And they're right. LeAnna has good self-esteem.

Self-esteem is self-regard, how much you cherish and appreciate being you. It's the "price tag" you place on yourself. Are you a valuable commodity, or a "markdown"?

It's all about a self picture. Our price tag advertises for others what we think of ourselves—and they will pretty much treat us accordingly. Think of it: When you're shopping, don't you handle a $100 blouse a lot more carefully than a $20 blouse? The way you communicate (your choice of words, your tone and style of relating, how well you listen), as well as how you present yourself (your appearance, your manners), are just a few of the many telltale signs of how much you value, honor and respect yourself. Psychologists say that self-esteem has a direct effect on all aspects of your health—mental, social and physical. Healthy self-esteem serves you well. Not so for low self-esteem. Teens with low self-esteem are more likely to do poorly in school, suffer from eating disorders and to engage in self-destructive behaviors, like smoking, drinking, doing drugs and being promiscuous.

Because the way you think of yourself is evident in everything you say and do, how you feel about yourself is often obvious to the people around you. What we think of ourselves becomes our "price tag."

"Just Me, Love Dan"

Because your self-regard is reflected in your behavior, other people can readily see what you think of yourself. In a workshop I conducted for teens some months ago, a seventeen-year-old guy told me that once when he wrote his girlfriend, Katerina, a letter and signed it "Just me, Love Dan" she gave the letter back to him, telling him she didn't like the way he signed it. "I'd like to think that I'm going out with someone who thinks more of himself than just me," she informed him. "When you sign your letters, 'just me,' I take it to mean you don't think of yourself as very special, so I must not be all that special either."

You see, to Dan, Katerina was absolutely the best thing in the world. He treasured her and was honored and so happy to be going out with her. "Why on earth would you think that?" he asked, completely surprised at her words. "Because," Katerina replied, "if you don't think very much of you, how could you possibly be going out with a really great girl, like me? I'd like to think of myself that way—as a really special person. But if you don't think much of you, how can you be worthy of me? I mean, I don't want to go out with a guy who thinks of himself as 'nobody special.'"

It's an interesting point. Obviously Dan's girlfriend thought Dan was special, special enough to be dating him, special enough to be her steady boyfriend. It made perfect sense to Katerina that her boyfriend should consider himself worthy enough for her. Because Katerina thinks of herself as a terrific girl, it's a put-down to Katerina for Dan to consider himself a "just me," a "nobody special."

"After thinking about it," Dan told me, "I realized Katerina was right. I decided to stop talking (and writing) about myself in a way that made me look as though I am not a person who appreciates how good it is to have Katerina for a girlfriend—and how good it is to have me as my own friend, someone I admire and speak well of. It was a valuable lesson. Just as I sign my letters to Katerina with 'Love, Dan' to let her know that my feelings for her are positive and loving, the words I say to me should be as positive and loving, too."

Self-Esteem: Building Beauty from the Inside Out

As Katerina explained to Dan, self-esteem shows how you feel about yourself. It's the level of your self-confidence—how bright, personable, caring, witty and wonderful you think you are. This self-picture affects how you care for your health and value your well-being; how meticulous you are in your grooming; the friends you choose; the goals you set and achieve. It also makes a major difference in how happy you are!

There was a guy in my high school, Brent, who found it all too easy to belittle others. "Another bad hair day, Susan?" he'd snicker to a classmate of ours if her hair wasn't particularly as neat and well-groomed as she usually kept it. "Nothing zinc wouldn't cure," was a favorite phrase of his when a classmate had scored low on a test or quiz or done poorly on a homework assignment. This comment was usually followed by Brent waving his high marks or good score in the air for the other students to see. Brent always made others feel insignificant and pointed out how smart he was. Unfortunately Brent's proclamations of his good marks and talents always came at another's expense.

Every now and then someone would remark that Brent "really felt sure of himself." In fact, the opposite was true. If Brent had felt better about himself, then he wouldn't have found it necessary to be so critical of others.

With a healthy self-esteem, far from being conceited or self-centered, you have an authentic sense of self. This means you understand that you are human. You have good days. You have bad days. You have ordinary days. You are awesome and capable of greatness. You are vulnerable and will sometimes fail at things. Allowing for both the ups and downs, taking the good with the bad, gives you a more realistic sense of self, a compassionate sense of self. If you can imagine and accept this range of traits within yourself, then you can imagine and accept this range within others. This is what it means to "understand" and "show consideration to" others.

The Benefits of a Healthy Self-Esteem

- The higher your self-esteem, the more accepting and honoring you are of yourself. You like yourself. You want you as a friend.

- The higher your self-esteem, the more you take care of yourself. Because you value your health and wellness, you do the things that protect them.

- The more you appreciate yourself, the less likely it is that you will compare yourself with others. Your measuring stick for judging yourself is within.

- The higher your self-esteem, the better able you will be to find ways to get along well with others. Teens with a healthy self-esteem form close relationships with people who respect and value them.

- The higher your self-esteem, the more likely you will treat others with respect and fairness, since self-respect is the basis of respect for others.

- The higher your self-esteem, the more you will attract others who enjoy their lives and are working to their potential. People with low self-esteem tend to seek low-self-esteem friends, who also think poorly of themselves.

- The higher your self-esteem, the better able you are to cope with the ups and downs of life. Teens with a healthy self-esteem have a realistic view of their strengths and weaknesses and maintain a positive attitude when they fail at a task.

- The higher your self-esteem, the more likely you will be to think about what you want out of life, the more ambitious you will be in going after it and the more likely you will be to achieve it.

- The higher your self-esteem, the more you will confront

obstacles and fears, rather than avoid them. Low-esteem individuals see problems as grounds for quitting and often say to themselves, "I give up."

- The higher your self-esteem, the more able you are to recognize your own worth and achievements without a constant need for approval from others.

- The higher your self-esteem, the more responsibility you take for your own actions. When you recognize that you are off course, you are more likely to self-correct, to stop going in a negative direction and begin anew.

- The higher your self-esteem, the more willing you are to hang in there, even when the going gets tough. Because you persist, your chances for experiencing success are greater. The more success you experience, the less likely it is that you will feel devastated or deflated by periodic setbacks.

- The higher your self-esteem, the happier you are. And a happy person with a big smile is a beautiful person who makes other people want to be around her.

Can You Change Your Self-Esteem?

Yes. You can change your self-esteem, but it's not a yo-yo. You don't just wake up one day with a high self-esteem or a low self-esteem. It's not like having a good hair day and a bad hair day. On some days, it seems like your hair has a mind of its own and it won't do what you want no matter what, but self-esteem isn't like that.

Your self-esteem is the whole picture of how you see yourself. Experts say that this picture is the product of about a year's worth of "pictures." Here's the way it works. Let's say that you are an average student in math. For most of your ninth-grade year, you received Cs. If this is the case, when friends ask you if you are "good at math," chances are you will say, "average." So if you get an A on a test during this year when you see yourself as an average student, you will be very happy (or think it was "just luck"), but the one A is unlikely to change your mind about being an "average" student in math.

Now, let's say that you have been getting Cs for the first three months of ninth-grade math, and then, for the next three months you have been earning mostly As. How do you see yourself, as a C student or an A student? If you see yourself as earning As more and more consistently, your view of yourself as a C student is going to change. And that's the way it is with esteem. If the picture you had of yourself in the past was of someone who doesn't speak up for herself, as someone in the habit of putting herself down, of not having friends (you get the idea), but now you see yourself as working on your goals, as being a courteous and conscientious person who is slowly but surely gaining the respect of others (yourself included), then the image of yourself is changing.

What wonderful news! We can improve our self-esteem.

From Bad to Good, from Bad to Worse

Naturally there's a catch. Self-esteem can go from good to bad, too. Using the example above, things could be reversed. If you have been a good student in math for awhile, but for the last half-year things have changed and you are now getting lower and lower grades, then chances are you are going to lose confidence in yourself as being a good student in math class.

The same concept applies to your ideas of how attractive you are. Maybe your overall sense of your attractiveness up until now was pretty good. But then the stage of adolescence begins with all of its growth demands—enormous physical changes move your body from a child to an adult, accompanied by erratic mood shifts and ups and downs, highs and lows. All these new and puzzling changes can leave you wondering if you're okay and if you are all that attractive and desirable to others, especially if you're trying to get used to the "new you."

The news is still good: You can work to improve the image you have of yourself. This holds true in almost every area, whether it be your image of your body as healthy, fit and attractive, or your image of yourself as a student, a friend, or a son or daughter.

Because a healthy self-esteem is so important, caring for it is one of the most important things you can do. A healthy self-esteem is achieved by actively participating in your life in a meaningful way. For example, you make a pact with yourself to be your own best friend, and not to say or do those things that do not represent you. You take responsibility for your choices, actions and behavior. You work toward those goals that are important to you. You think about what you want out of life—and work toward bringing your ideals to life.

Self-esteem is a consequence of your actions. The more you set and achieve worthwhile goals in all areas of your life, the better you respect and honor yourself.

How to Improve Your Self-Esteem

Because self-esteem is so important, you need to know how to take care of yours. A healthy self-esteem is a result, a consequence of seeing yourself doing positive things in positive ways in five key areas:

1. Your sense of purpose

2. Your emotional security (intrinsic worth)

3. Your friendships and associations with others

4. Your safety

5. Your achievements (and sense of being a capable person)

Throughout this book, you'll learn more about how to care for yourself in each of these areas, but in a nutshell, here are the things you can do to have a "good reputation" with yourself.

- Believe that you have a right to live a happy and fulfilling life.

- Take good care of your body. Don't take risks that could put your safety and your health in jeopardy (such as using drugs and alcohol).

- Get to know and understand yourself and make friends with the face in the mirror. Treat yourself with respect. Don't put yourself down with sarcasm or hurtful words. (Others will take your lead and treat you as you treat yourself. Remember, you are the one setting this standard.)

- Make choices consistent with values you know to be good and right, those you can be proud to stand up for.

- Set worthy goals and strive to achieve them.

- Develop a "can-do" attitude, but accept that just as you have strengths, you have weaknesses. Everyone has both.

- Take time out regularly to be alone with yourself so that you can listen to yourself and ponder your inner thoughts and feelings. Cultivate activities you can enjoy by yourself, like crafts, reading or an individual sport. The goal is to become your very best friend, to truly enjoy your own company.

- Learn effective ways to manage the way(s) you respond to stress.

- Practice your faith. Faith is about the timeless truths and provides leadership to your heart and soul—the core of your being.

- Read broadly and expose yourself to great minds. This allows you to examine your own assumptions, and to grow and become wise. Refuse to narrow and close your mind so that assumptions are never examined.

- Reach out to others to talk about how things are going for you. You will find others know what you are talking about. They've been there. People around you understand and are willing to cut you some slack, especially if you are good-natured and courteous. It's only natural that sometimes you'll mess up. When this happens, admit it, talk about it, apologize for your shortcomings, and then vow to do better. This shows maturity. And you'll feel better about yourself and more confident in getting through the next "crisis"—and there will be many. That's just the way life is when you're a teen.

You Don't Have to Go It Alone

Learning how to cope effectively with your life can help you be a happy person—and that's the goal. But sometimes the stress and strains are simply too big for you to handle alone. Asking for help when you need it is a sign of strength and an attribute of inner beauty—and a mark of a person with good self-esteem.

Should you be facing struggles that seem overwhelming, rather than suffer alone or resort to doing things that are self-destructive, I urge you to confide in a best friend, as well as an adult you trust. (This is especially true in the case of physical or sexual abuse, suicidal feelings, eating disorders, depression, pregnancy or using drugs or alcohol.) Remember that parents, teachers and other professionals such as school nurses or counselors were once teens (and many are the parents of teens) and know what it feels like to be unsure of yourself, to have fears and anxieties about coping with life in general.

It can be helpful to remember that if you have had a bad experience when an adult seemed aloof to your needs, or even broke your trust, this is generally the exception to the rule. Trust that adults have the best interest of teens at heart and want to help you make the best choices in dealing with the things going on in your life. And here's a secret I'd like to let you in on. It can be scary to tell your parents that you feel in over your head on something—like experimenting with drugs or drinking or suspecting you may be pregnant—for fear that they will be upset with you.

The truth is, they probably will be upset in the beginning because they may be as overwhelmed and frightened as you. But even if you think they will be upset, even if you feel you have let your parents down, tell them anyway because once they work through their own fears and feelings, most always they will get to work to help you sort things out. After all, your well-being is their number-one concern, so brave their reaction and know that in the end, your parents usually are the ones who know what's best for you and will do all they can to help you. And once your parents are on board, they will help you see it through to the end. I know this. I've experienced it firsthand as a teen myself, and have had hundreds and hundreds of teens tell me how turning to their parents, as difficult as it may have been, was the best thing they could have done.

And remember, especially when life seems particularly stressful, it's time to be extra good to yourself—get adequate rest, eat properly and get the exercise your body needs to burn off tension. "Cool" is a decidedly wonderful aspect of beauty, one that begins on the inside and radiates out.

If You've Got It Together . . .

As you can see, a healthy self-esteem is pretty important to that "price tag" you set for yourself. When you have a healthy self-esteem, it is often so noticeable that it prompts others to remark, "You really have your act together!"

Why is self-esteem such a valued commodity? Because a positive sense of self is a sure contribution to your beauty.

4

From "Me" to "You"

When we seek to discover the best in others, we somehow bring out the best in ourselves. —William Arthur Ward

Harmony: It Takes Two to Tango

Self-esteem is a focus on self and your own needs. Learning how to nurture yourself, being attentive to your own needs and interests, leads to a sense of being "in sync" within your life. This internal sense of confidence and peace provides a feeling of contentment and harmony. But excessive self-absorption creates a profound sense of loss, of alienation and isolation from ourselves. Like the expression goes, "No man is an island."

We need others.

As we grow in self-awareness and understand the importance of feeling at peace with ourselves, we move from concentrating solely on the self and its internal experience of harmony, to an outward sense of harmony with others. Having developed skills for seeing into yourself, and having learned to appreciate what you see, you can now apply these skills of "seeing into me," to "seeing into you." It's an important venture.

As we turn our focus outward, moving from "me" to "you" adds yet another dimension to our inner contentment. It makes us happy. The more harmonious the relationships we have with others, the greater our inner satisfaction—in a word, happiness.

What Makes You Most Happy?

What do you think is the greatest source of happiness for people? When you think about those times when you are truly happy and content, to what do you attribute it? Is it because you have just accomplished something, like acing a big test? Or is it because you are in a really "good space" with your family and friends?

In Taste Berries for Teens: Inspirational Short Stories and Encouragement on Life, Love, Friendships and Tough Issues, a book I coauthored with my mother, we asked nearly six thousand teens "What makes you happy?" Teens of all ages and from diverse backgrounds said "feeling close to their friends and parents" was a source of their feeling content. As it turns out, the same thing is true for adults! When ABC television—in conjunction with an hour-long program on happiness—polled the American public, asking them, "What accounts for the greatest happiness in life?" Their answer? Close relationships. This was followed by control over one's life, challenging and fulfilling work, a sense of optimism, faith in God, and a sense of purpose. Money and material things—such as a great house or cars and such—did not show up in the top six on the list, contrary to what many might suspect.

For teens and adults as well, feeling close—a sense of community and connection—is a rich source of happiness.

The Bunny-Love Experiment

This connection with others is also good for our health! This was demonstrated accidentally in a research project using rabbits as subjects. Researchers couldn't understand why within a large pen of bunnies, noticeable differences surfaced in the bunnies after about a month or so of being together. Some bunnies appeared to be in better health than others; for example, their coats were thick and shiny. Some bunnies were more social and playful, while—others began to withdraw, huddle alone or shy away from the others.

Because all bunnies were fed the same diet, scientists really couldn't account for the differences. Baffled, the directors of the research looked into it. What they discovered was an amazingly simple explanation. Each and every day, a night lab worker had been playing with some of the bunnies, giving certain ones his attention and affection as he was cleaning the lab.

Once the researchers learned this, they separated the bunnies into two groups, this time deliberately giving certain rabbits more attention and affection than the others. Sure enough, the bunnies receiving the affection and attention once again showed better overall health, and were more social—romping more playfully with each other than the others. Obviously, TLC (tender loving care) is good for a bunny's health and sense of play!

Like bunnies, people "thrive" on attention and care, too.

Getting—and Giving—All the TLC You Need

Think about those people who are your anchors, those you can count on to be there for you, whether to cheer you on or to help you mend an aching heart. For me it's my parents, friends and grandparents—especially my Grandma Burres. I think of her often, and when I do, usually she'll call. When I call her, she'll almost always say to me, "Oh, 'Jennicans'" (one of her three nicknames for me—and one that only she is allowed to use!), "I was just thinking of you!" Connecting with my grandma is always a good feeling. But she also has a way about her of being so solid, so strong, so able to make me feel whole.

When I was growing up, at those times when my mother was "out of juice," as she would say, she'd go to spend a day or two with her parents. "Spending even a day with them is like going to the well!" she would report. "Whenever I'm in need of mothering, no one puts me back together quite like my mom and dad do!" As a child, I didn't really understand what she meant when she said this, but I do know that when my mother returned home, she was peaceful, joyful and serene. Being with her parents provided her with a source of strength unlike the other people she needed in her life. Now I fully understand the importance of being with people who make us feel good about ourselves, who provide us with a safe place to share our innermost thoughts and needs, and who love us unconditionally. My grandmother is that special to me, as is my mother. There are others of course, but I realize the importance of these two significant people in my life.

Family—Cookies and Milk for the Heart

Family is a most important source of TLC. As a teenager, you may not always feel that your parents are a number-one source, but usually they are. I know when I'm at odds about something with my mom or dad, even though I act strong and pretend it's not that big of a deal, the truth is, it's very upsetting to me. When I was in high school (and still, even now at twenty-five), an argument with my parents was disheartening. If I disagree with them, and even if I'm sure I'm right in going with a choice I've made over another one they've counseled me to select, I feel uneasy, like there's a piece of my life that isn't in harmony. And of course, that disharmony is upsetting. My parents and I have a close relationship, and I love and respect them, so when we're on the outs, when there's discord, it doesn't feel good.

My friends feel the same. Jaime, a seventeen-year-old friend said it this way: "If I'm in an argument with my parents, it isn't like I can go to school and just forget about it. I'll be sitting in class, not really paying attention to what is going on because I'll be off in my mind, still thinking about the argument. Rather than concentrating on what the teacher is saying, I'm still involved: What were my parents thinking? Why did they say what they did (or didn't)? Then I wonder why I said what I did—or why I didn't say what I should have! And then I try to decide on a good time and a good way to reopen a conversation with them so I can go where I wanted, or get what I wanted or have what I wanted in the first place!

"So I sit in class, planning a new strategy, and playing through every possible response—several times. Of course, this means that I'm still not paying attention to what's going on in class. This upsets me too, so then I get worked up all over again. Sometimes I take out my frustration on my teachers, or my friends by being impatient with them, or I pass my anxiety off on them—even though I don't mean to. I'm not the only one this happens to. My friends feel upset too when it happens to them. What I'm learning is that feeling close to my parents is important to me. I want to have a good relationship with them."

Many teens feel like Jamie. And many teens also want to be close to their siblings. Believe it or not, brothers and sisters are our number-one fans. My friend Alicia and her younger sister bicker between themselves all the time, but when it comes to defending each other, no one is more loyal than they are to each other. So, take good care of your relationship with your family and work to be in a harmonious relationship with them. Of all my friends, those who have good relationships with their families are happier than those who are constantly on the outs with them. As for me, I always feel happiest when I'm in a "good place" with my family—and with my friends.

Friends—Pizza for Life!

What would life be like if you didn't have good friends? For me, I can't even imagine it! Like teens everywhere, I rely on harmony with my friends as an important source of contentment.

For me, a good friend is someone I can count on, someone with whom I can relax and just hang out, have fun and share my innermost thoughts—deep, dark secrets, lofty and noble goals, or my hopes, joys and fears. I know a friend is a good friend when I feel that with her it is okay—a safe space—to share my deepest thoughts and needs—without worry of being judged, criticized or made to feel silly for feeling the way I do. Friends cheer each other on, laugh and cry together, and just plain commiserate and listen to each other. That's why friends are friends.

Friends help you to grow into being who you are and allow you to reveal those parts of yourself that you may be meeting for the first time. What a wonderful gift. From coping with the death of a loved one to dealing with the everyday ups and downs of life—like sharing a secret too good to keep, or mourning a breakup with a special someone—friends are important in our lives.

Having people who are "there for us" as a source of strength, support and rejuvenation is not only special, but important. Take a moment to think about who provides this source of comfort to you. Hold these relationships close to your heart and protect them by staying in touch and showing your support, remembering to offer them comfort in return.

TLC Is a Two-Way Street

The key to being a good friend is fairly simple: It's reaching out to show others you are thoughtful and considerate, and a person who strives to create harmony among others. How? By seeing the good in others and letting them know how much they mean to you.

When you help others feel good about themselves, you help them see you as someone special to them. If you want to test this principle, recall a time when someone made a comment that made you feel good about yourself. For example, just recently I had some red highlights added to my hair. A girl I work with noticed and said, "Oh, Jennifer! Your hair color is positively fabulous; it looks just great on you!" Her comment made me feel "positively fabulous" all day.

Share the joy.

There are many ways you can share good feelings with others. For example, if you notice a friend or classmate has a new haircut or is wearing her hair differently and it looks really good, you can say, "I really like your new hairstyle. It looks great on you!" If a friend (or parent or teacher) is in an especially good mood or is feeling excited about something, you can say, "Being in a good mood sure looks great on you!" If a friend or classmate has been working out, cheer them on with a good word of encouragement: "That jogging you've taken up is really paying off! You look really good." If someone has just taken a leap to wearing a new style of clothes or color of makeup that works well for them, tell them about it. If someone is having a bad day, stop and listen. Show empathy.

Helping others feel good about themselves will not only win you friends, but it will make you feel better about yourself. Try it and see! Open doors for people young and old, offer to help, say a kind word, pick up a piece of trash even though it wasn't you who discarded it. Volunteer in your community. Be a person who likes people. We live in a world with others. I love a saying from one of my mother's books, Taste-Berry Tales: "It is our obligation—as much as it is our honor—to help others see their lives in a positive light." I believe that. I know from experience that helping others is a most important way to see yourself as a loving and generous person. And feeling good about yourself is a positive contribution to your beauty.

"Play with Him"

From saving a lizard to building homes for Habitat for Humanity, there are many ways to get involved in the lives of others. Some of these can be as simple as being good to the people we meet in our everyday lives. I remember being with my mother on a television interview for a recent book. Actress Annie Potts was also a guest on the show. When asked how she managed her professional life along with being the mother of three young children, she listed several things that helped her, one of them being her children's looking out for each other. One of her remarks especially stood out. She said, "I tell my children to love each other, and then I take my older son aside and say, 'Be good to your little brother. Play with him.'" When I heard that, I thought, how loving—and how simple. Playing with his little brother when their mother was away was the ultimate show of taking a loving, caretaking role in the responsibility of seeing that the little boy was a happy little camper when Mommy was gone.

Believe that others need you. If ever you doubt it:

- Help someone who is ill, infirm or broken-hearted. Feel their vulnerability and hold it close to your heart. Feel how good it is to provide strength when another needs it.

- Assist someone. If you see someone drop something, offer help gathering things. Watch the gratitude on that person's face.

- Call out in a friendly, comforting tone to a stray, lost or wounded animal. Feel the tug of your heart, and the tear within your eyes, as you offer compassion and extend human caring for the creatures nature has provided for our overseeing and protecting. Diligently care for your own pet. Allow yourself to feel the love your pet gives to you.

- Compliment others, even those you don't know, on how nice they look, whether it be the smile on their face, or the clothes they are wearing.

In doing these things, you'll find goodwill produces harmony. Inner harmony is a most luminous facet of beauty. There's nothing more radiant than an inner harmony that displays itself in sparkling eyes, a friendly smile and a sense of self that is generous enough to care about others.

5

The Beauty of Purpose and Passion

Doing quality work—that's what brings you self-respect. —Sadie Delany, age 107, first African American woman to teach home economics in New York City schools

Patricia Hill Burnett

I have a photo of me with my friend Patricia Hill Burnett (author of True Colors: An Artist's Journey from Beauty Queen to Feminist); she is so vibrant: Her smile is generous, her eyes sparkle, she is sitting tall and looking directly at you! Dressed impeccably as always, in stylish and vibrantly colored clothes, and wearing beautiful jewelry that compliments her apparel, she is a picture of beauty. All of this gives off an air that here is a smart and classy woman, a woman who is in command of herself. And she is!

A large part of Patricia's vibrancy comes from her active involvement in her life—and work. And this is one of the great secrets of real beauty. A prime source of "confidence" and "motivation" and "sass" and "spunk" and "vitality"—all traits we admire and revere in others—emanates from feeling purposeful.

Having something important that you like to do gives meaning to your life and is the birthplace for the inner qualities of zest and zeal. In Patricia's case, she is a gifted artist, a painter who has painted the portraits of presidents and other world leaders and dignitaries, everyone from Indira Gandhi to Margaret Thatcher. Just look at her exquisite talent!

Patricia actively pursues goals that are important to her. Though she has had a lifetime of achievements, she isn't sitting back or resting on past performance. Nor is Patricia thinking of retiring—even though she is eighty years old!

The photo of the two of us together was taken this past year. Patricia, a first runner-up Miss America in 1942, born in 1920, is one of the most beautiful women ever. Still!

People like Patricia show us the importance of purposeful activity in our lives. It's part of what gives her such a sense of presence. I have always believed that a goal of work is to be able to make our joys our job, and Patricia has done just that. Patricia is an example of radiance that stems from her work as a source of satisfaction. When you are busy working toward something important, you feel purposeful.

Setting and achieving worthwhile goals is the key.

A Goal Is Like a Road Map

A goal is like having a map. If you know the direction you should be heading, you know where to focus your time and energy. Channeling your efforts in a single direction can keep you on track so that you actually get to your destination. How many times have you heard the expression, "I got sidetracked"? Goals keep you on track so you can accomplish your dreams. You know where you should be spending your time, and you have made plans to do the things you need to do to accomplish your desires. For example, suppose that you are going to run in a mile-long race. If you don't record on your calendar the date of the race, and then make a plan to assure that you do well in it—like eating the right foods, getting into shape, and warming up before the race—you just might tumble out of bed one morning and say, "Gee, I can't believe the race is today!" If you'd not made plans to do well in it, you may just feel awful when you are through—assuming you do finish!

Here are some helpful tips for setting goals:

1. Be specific in your goals. Goals that are specific, as opposed to ambiguous, provide better direction. For example, rather than, "Start working out," say, "I'm going to exercise three times a week."

2. Set a timeline and target dates for accomplishment. For example, "I'm going to exercise each Monday and Thursday in my physical education class and go to the workout center with my mom on Saturdays."

3. Break your goal into manageable parts. We call these subgoals. For example:

Goal: To get adequate sleep each night.
Subgoal: Will not drink caffeinated soft drinks at night.
Subgoal: Will not play rock or heavy metal CDs at least one hour before going to bed.
Subgoal: Get started on my homework right after school instead of waiting until the last minute.

4. Break your goals into realistic and manageable timelines so that you know what you should be doing and when. For example:

Major Goal: To buff up.
Subgoal: To tone my muscles.
Monthly Goal: Work out ten times.
Weekly Goals: Commit to a rigorous workout in gym class each Monday and Wednesday.
-Work out at the Family Fitness Center on Saturday with Mom (or a friend).
-Take my dog Bowser for a ten minute run (or walk) after school instead of goading my little sister to do it for me.

5. Put your goals in writing. Doing so helps you clearly identify what you want, and it increases your personal commitment to your goals.

6. Keep a copy of your goal plan in sight and refer to it often. For example, if your goal is to exercise each Monday, Thursday and

Saturday, tape a copy of that goal on the inside of your notebook, so you won't schedule yourself to do something else instead—like make plans with friends that keep you from your goal! If your goal is to stop eating junk food, put that goal on the refrigerator and maybe on the inside of your notebook so that when you pass the snack dispenser you will be more easily swayed to purchase an apple instead of a candy bar.

7. Guidelines for Setting Goals

It's really not enough to have one goal, nor is it realistic to have twenty goals and to think that you will actually accomplish all of them. Six categories of goals are shown below, with an added "other" area so you can create any other category you might want to work on. If you have one goal and one sub-goal in each area, you will have more than enough to do; yet you will not be so overwhelmed that you simply abandon doing the things you would like to achieve. Write down your goal and the primary subgoal in each category.

Creating Goals of Your Own

Relationships
(Goals in your relationships with parents, friends, teachers, others.)
Goal: _____

Subgoal: _____

Learning and Education
(What would you like to know more about? What skills do you want to develop? To what formal education do you aspire?)
Goal: _____

Subgoal: _____

Job or Career Satisfaction
(Goals for getting a job or for preparing for what you want to do as a career.)
Goal: _____

Subgoal: _____

Leisure-Time Pursuits
(Goals for your leisure time and activities: hobbies, sports and other interests you want to develop.)
Goal: _____

Subgoal: _____

Status and Respect
(To which groups do you want to belong? To what extent do you want to be respected by others? From whom do you want respect?)
Goal: _____

Subgoal: _____

Spiritual Growth
(Goals for peace of mind, your search for spiritual meaning.)
Goal: _____

Subgoal: _____

Others
(A goal that may not fit into the other categories, but is important to you.)
Goal: _____

Subgoal: _____

The More I Try, the Luckier I Get: Achievement Is a Source of Satisfaction

The more you accomplish your goals, the greater your sense of satisfaction. The greater your sense of satisfaction, the greater your sense of self. The greater your sense of self, the happier you are. The happier you are, the greater your inner beauty. And as you've learned throughout this book, that inner beauty keeps bubbling until it comes to the surface!

Other Books for Young Adults

Health & Fitness for Teens

Jennifer L. Youngs

Health & Fitness for Teens covers a most essential topic for teens: having a healthy body, liking your body and being fit. It's also a time of constant change. We can feel like we're just getting to know who we are when suddenly we are someone totally different. This book uncovers some of the myths teens have for comparing themselves to a standard other than their own, and covers some very important ground on how to best take care of themselves so as to look and feel their very best.

ISBN: 978-1-940784-33-5• ePub: 978-1-940784-32-8

Lessons from the Gym For Young Adults

5 Secrets for Being in Control of Your Life

Chris Cucchiara

As a teen, Chris Cucchiara's life was a mess. Then he discovered the gym and he was transformed inside and out. Says Chris, "The gym taught me discipline, which led to achieving goals, which started a cycle of success." A much-admired high-performance coach for teens, in this book, Chris share his guiding principles on how to: develop mental toughness (a life without fear, stress, and anger); become and stay healthy and fit; build an "athlete for life" mentality that stresses excellence; and, set and achieve goals that matter.

ISBN: 978-1-936332-38-0 • ePub: 978-1-936332-34-2

Lessons from the Gym For Young Adults

Workbook

Chris Cucchiara

A SUCCESS WORKBOOK FOR YOUNG ADULTS (ages 12-20) Do you lack self-confidence or have a difficult time making decisions? Do you sometimes wonder what is worth doing? Do you ever have a tough time feeling a sense of purpose and belonging? Chris shares his expertise of mastering success principles and shows you how to: Discover your real passion and purpose in life, which provides the drive, ambition and determination to overcome your limiting beliefs, fears, stress, and anger; Feel more in control of your life; Build your confidence and self-esteem; Build an athlete for life mentality that stresses leadership and excellence as a mindset; and, Stay motivated and set and achieve goals.

ISBN: 978-1-940784-16-8

Law of Attraction for Teens
How to Get More of the Good Stuff, and Get Rid of the Bad Stuff!

Christopher Combates

Whether it's getting better grades, creating better relationships, getting into college, or attracting a special someone, the Law of Attraction works! Aligning goals with your intentions enables you to create a better life. Written for teens, this engaging book will help teens to set purposeful goals, and to think, act, andcommunicate in the most positive way possible.

ISBN: 978-1-936332-29-8• ePub: 978-1-936332-30-4

Fastest Man in the World
The Tony Volpentest Story

Tony Volpentest
Foreword by Ross Perot

Tony Volpentest, a four-time Paralympic gold medalist and five-time world champion sprinter, is a 2012 nominee for the Olympic Hall of Fame. This inspirational story details his being born without feet, to holding records as the fastest sprinter in the world.

"This inspiring story is about the thrill of victory to be sure—winning gold—but it is also a reminder about human potential: the willingness to push ourselves beyond the ledge of our own imagination. A powerfully inspirational story." —**Charlie Huebner, United States Olympic Committee**

ISBN: 978-1-940784-07-6 • ePub: 978-1-940784-08-3

The Girl Who Gave Her Wish Away

Sharon Babineau
Foreword by Craig Kielburger

The Children's Wish Foundation approached lovely thirteen-year-old Maddison Babineau just after she received her cancer diagnosis. "You can have anything," they told her, "a Disney cruise? The chance to meet your favorite movie star? A five thousand dollar shopping spree?"

Maddie knew exactly what she wanted. She had recently been moved to tears after watching a television program about the plight of orphaned children. Maddie's wish? To ease the suffering of these children half-way across the world. Despite the ravishing cancer, she became an indefatigable fundraiser for "her children." In The Girl Who Gave Wish Away, her mother reveals Maddie's remarkable journey of providing hope and future to the village children who had filled her heart.

A special story, heartwarming and reassuring.

ISBN: 978-1-936332-96-0 • ePub: 978-1-936332-97-7

GPS YOUR BEST LIFE
Charting Your Destination and Getting There in Style

Charmaine Hammond and Debra Kasowski
Foreword by Jack Canfield

A most useful guide to charting and traversing the many options that lay before you.

"A perfect book for servicing your most important vehicle: yourself. No matter where you are in your life, the concepts and direction provided in this book will help you get to a better place. It's a must read." —**Ken Kragen, author of** *Life Is a Contact Sport*, **and organizer of** *We Are the World*, **and** *Hands Across America*, **and other historic humanitarian events**

ISBN: 978-1-936332-26-7 • ePub: 978-1-936332-41-0

News Girls Don't Cry
Melissa McCarty

Today the host of ORA TV's Newsbreaker, and now calling Larry King her boss, Melissa McCarty worked her way up through the trenches of live television news. But she was also running away from her past, one of growing up in the roughest of neighborhoods, watching so many she knew—including her brother—succumb to drugs, gangs, and violence. It was a past that forced her to be tough and streetwise, traits that in her career as a popular television newscaster, would end up working against her.

Every tragic story she covered was a grim reminder of where she'd been. But the practiced and restrained emotion given to the camera became her protective armor even in her private life where she was unable to let her guard down—a demeanor that damaged both her personal and professional relationships. In News Girls Don't Cry, McCarty confronts the memory-demons of her past, exploring how they hardened her—and how she turned it all around.

An inspiring story of overcoming adversity, welcoming second chances, and becoming happy and authentic.

"A battle between personal success and private anguish, a captivating brave tale of a woman's drive to succed and her tireless struggle to keep her family intact. The reader is pulled into Melissa's story... an honest account of the common battle of addiction." —**Susan Hendricks, CNN Headline News Anchor**

ISBN: 978-1-936332-69-4 • ePub: 978-1-936332-70-0

Electric Living
The Science behind the Law of Attraction

Kolie Crutcher

An electrical engineer by training, Crutcher applies his in-depth knowledge of electrical engineering principles and practical engineering experience detailing the scientific explanation of why human beings become what they think. A practical, step-by-step guide to help you harness your thoughts and emotions so that the Law of Attraction will benefit you.

ISBN: 978-1-936332-58-8 • ePub: 978-1-936332-59-5

Karmic Alibi
Gaining EXPEDIENT Wisdom by Leaving Your Excuses Behind

Patricia Karen Gagic

Karma is a potent law of the universe. Karma, literally meaning "action," is the sum of your intentional and deliberate consciousness, which prescribes your thoughts and thus determines your actions.

Just as positive thoughts initiate positive outcomes, negative thoughts create angst. The "wisdom" of your Karma is yours alone; you cannot experience someone else's Karma.

In Karmic Alibi, expert Patricia Gagic shares how you can influence the sovereignty of your Karma. By mastering the "five radical degrees of life" you can expedite the wisdom of your Karma so as to live in a state of joyful and purpose-filled abundance emotionally, physically and spiritually—which is your divine right.

In this soulful and most insightful book, Patricia examines her own beliefs and describes how she transformed them. By using examples from her life, and thanks to the trail markers she leaves along the way, she makes it easier for each of us to create the life we wish to live, too.

ISBN: 978-1-940784-29-8 • ePub: 978-1-940784-30-4

On Toby's Terms
Charmaine Hammond

On Toby's Terms is an endearing story of a beguiling creature who teaches his owners that, despite their trying to teach him how to be the dog they want, he is the one to lay out the terms of being the dog he needs to be. This insight would change their lives forever.

"This is a captivating, heartwarming story and we are very excited about bringing it to film." —**Steve Hudis, Producer**

ISBN: 978-0-9843081-4-9 • ePub: 978-1-936332-15-1

The Story of Millard and Linda Fuller, Founders of Habitat for Humanity and The Fuller Center for Housing

Bettie B. Youngs

Everyone has heard of Habitat for Humanity, the faith-based housing initiative that has built homes for more than a million of the world's poor. Many are familiar with its founders, Millard and Linda Fuller. But few know the amazing love story behind the movement—a story that began accidentally and will conclude in a world forever changed by its impact.

By age 29, Millard Fuller was a self-made millionaire. But that success came at a cost. He never took a family vacation, had kids he barely knew, and a lonely wife who was about to leave him. Ultimately, realizing that he was about to lose what really mattered, Fuller reconciled with his wife and rearranged his priorities.

In 1965, the Fullers gave away their personal fortune and dedicated their lives to serving others, eventually founding Habitat for Humanity in 1976. In this capacity, the Fullers traveled the globe, receiving the praise of prime ministers and presidents, sharing meals with prisoners, and appealing for funds and volunteers. More important than any accolade or award were the homes they built and the hope they gave. The Fullers have done more for the cause of housing the poor than any other couple in history.

Eventually, a struggle for the reins of the most beloved nonprofit of our times would result in the firing of Millard and Linda by Habitat International's board of directors. This certainly didn't mean the end to their vision—the Fullers would rebound, continuing to support local Habitat affiliates and beginning The Fuller Center for Housing, determined to pursue their dream of building for people everywhere simple, decent places to live.

ISBN: 978-0-9882848-8-3 • ePub: 978-1-936332-53-3

Amazing Adventures of a Nobody

Leon Logothetis

From the Hit Television Series Aired in 100 Countries!

Tired of his disconnected life and uninspiring job, Leon Logothetis leaves it all behind—job, money, home, even his cell phone—and hits the road with nothing but the clothes on his back and five dollars in his pocket, relying on the kindness of strangers and the serendipity of the open road for his daily keep. Masterful storytelling!

"A gem of a book; endearing, engaging and inspiring." —**Catharine Hamm, Los Angeles Times Travel Editor**

ISBN: 978-0-9843081-3-2 • ePub: 978-1-936332-51-9

Last Reader Standing
... The Story of a Man Who Learned to Read at 54

Archie Willard
with Colleen Wiemerslage

The day Archie lost his thirty-one year job as a laborer at a meat packing company, he was forced to confront the secret he had held so closely for most of his life: at the age of fifty-four, he couldn't read. For all his adult life, he'd been able to skirt around the issue. But now, forced to find a new job to support his family, he could no longer hide from the truth.

Last Reader Standing is the story of Archie's amazing—and often painful—journey of becoming literate at middle age, struggling with the newfound knowledge of his dyslexia. From the little boy who was banished to the back of the classroom because the teachers labeled him "stupid," Archie emerged to becoming a national figure who continues to enlighten professionals into the world of the learning disabled. He joined Barbara Bush on stage for her Literacy Foundation's fundraisers where she proudly introduced him as "the man who took advantage of a second chance and improved his life."

This is a touching and poignant story that gives us an eye-opening view of the lack of literacy in our society, and how important it is for all of us to have opportunity to become all that we can be—to have hope and go after our dreams.

At the age of eighty-two, Archie continues to work with literacy issues in medicine and consumerism.

"Archie . . . you need to continue spreading the word." —**Barbara Bush, founder of the Literacy Foundation, and First Lady and wife of George H. W. Bush, the 41st President of the United States**

ISBN: 978-1-936332-48-9 • ePub: 978-1-936332-50-2

The Aspiring Actor's Handbook

Molly Cheek and Debbie Zip

Concise and straightforward, The Aspiring Actor's Handbook is written for curious and aspiring actors to help them make informed decisions while pursuing this exciting career.

Veteran actresses Molly Cheek and Debbie Zipp have culled the wit and wisdom of a wide array of successful actors, from Beth Grant to Dee Wallace, and collected the kind of mentoring perspective so many in the business wish they'd had when they were just starting out. Get insider information and real-life experiences and personal stories that range from how to get your foot in the door to becoming a career actor. Get the inside scoop from successful veteran actors on how to work with agents and unions; manage finances; prepare for auditions; cope with rejection—and success—and much more.

ISBN: 978-1-940784-12-0 • ePub: 978-1-940784-02-1

The Predatory Lies of Anorexia
A Survivor's Story

Abby D. Kelly

"I want...I want you to think I am the smartest, the thinnest, the most beautiful..."

With these words, Abby Kelly encapsulates the overwhelming struggle of her 15-year bout with anorexia. Abby lays bare the reality of anorexia, beginning in her teenage years, when the predatory lies of the disease took root in her psyche as she felt pressured from family and peers for not being "enough." In her quest for a greater sense of personal power, she concludes "I'll be 'more', but it will be on my terms."

Her reasoning is a classic example as to why and how eating disorders dig in and persist as long as they do.

From this new self-awareness, Abby targets her body as the agent to show others that she is disciplined and focused. She sets out to restrict her food intake and adheres to an extreme schedule of exercise. While others close to Abby see a person who is dangerously thin, Abby, in fact, derives a sense of personal achievement from her weight loss.

Abby exposes the battles, defeats, and ultimate triumph—taking the reader on a poignant odyssey from onset to recovery, including how she set out to fool the many who tried to help her, from dietitians to therapists, from one inpatient treatment center after another, and reveals not only the victim's suffering, but that of those who love her.

This raw and passionate story eloquently describes how Abby finally freed herself from this life-threatening condition, and how others can find courage and hope for recovery, too.

"This beautifully written book paints an exacting picture of Anorexia, one that is sure to help legions of those suffering from this most serious and life-threatening condition."
—Amy Dardis, founder and editor of Haven Journal

ISBN: 978-1-940784-17-5 • ePub: 978-1-940784-18-2

FOR MORE READING VISIT OUR WEBSITE AT:
www.BettieYoungsBooks.com

If you are unable to order this book from your local bookseller, or online from Amazon or Barnes & Noble, or from Wholesaler Baker & Taylor, or from Espresso, or, Read How You Want, you may order directly from the publisher at Sales@BettieYoungsBooks.com.